Help! I'm In Treble!

A Child's Introduction to Music

Music Book for Beginners
Children's Musical Instruction & Study

Speedy Publishing LLC

40 E. Main St. #1156

Newark, DE 19711

www.speedypublishing.com

Copyright 2018

In this book, we're going to talk about how to read music. So, let's get right to it!

Do you love music? Maybe you've listened to a particular song and wondered what the song looks like in sheet music.

If you want to learn how to play a musical instrument, then understanding how to read music when it's in written form is a valuable skill.

Sheet music is written using symbols. Just like words represent certain meanings, the symbols in sheet music represent the pitch, as well as the speed and beat of a particular song.

THE STAFF

THE BASIC NOTATION OF MUSIC

There are some basic symbols you need to understand in order to read music.

The **staff** is a collection of five lines in a horizontal position with four spaces between them. Each line and each space stands for a different pitch. Composers write music by using the staff. Higher notes appear higher on the staff.

The clef is a symbol that's used at the left-hand side of a specific staff. It represents the pitch of the notes that are written there.

There are four major types of clefs. The ones that are used most frequently are the treble clef and the bass clef.

The notes are a combination of the pitch and the length of time of a particular sound. Let's look at each of these important symbols in more detail.

THE STAFF

The staff for writing music has five lines. Between those lines there are four spaces. Each of the lines stands for a specific letter. The same is true with the spaces. The letters represent various pitches of sound.

The Staff
lines
5
4
3
2
1
spaces
4
3
2
1
STAFF

MUSIC NOTES

THE TREBLE CLEF

The treble clef and the bass clef are the two major clefs you'll need to be able to read in order to understand sheet music. Notice that the treble clef has this very ornamental symbol at the staff's left side that stands for the letter "g." It's also sometimes described as the G clef.

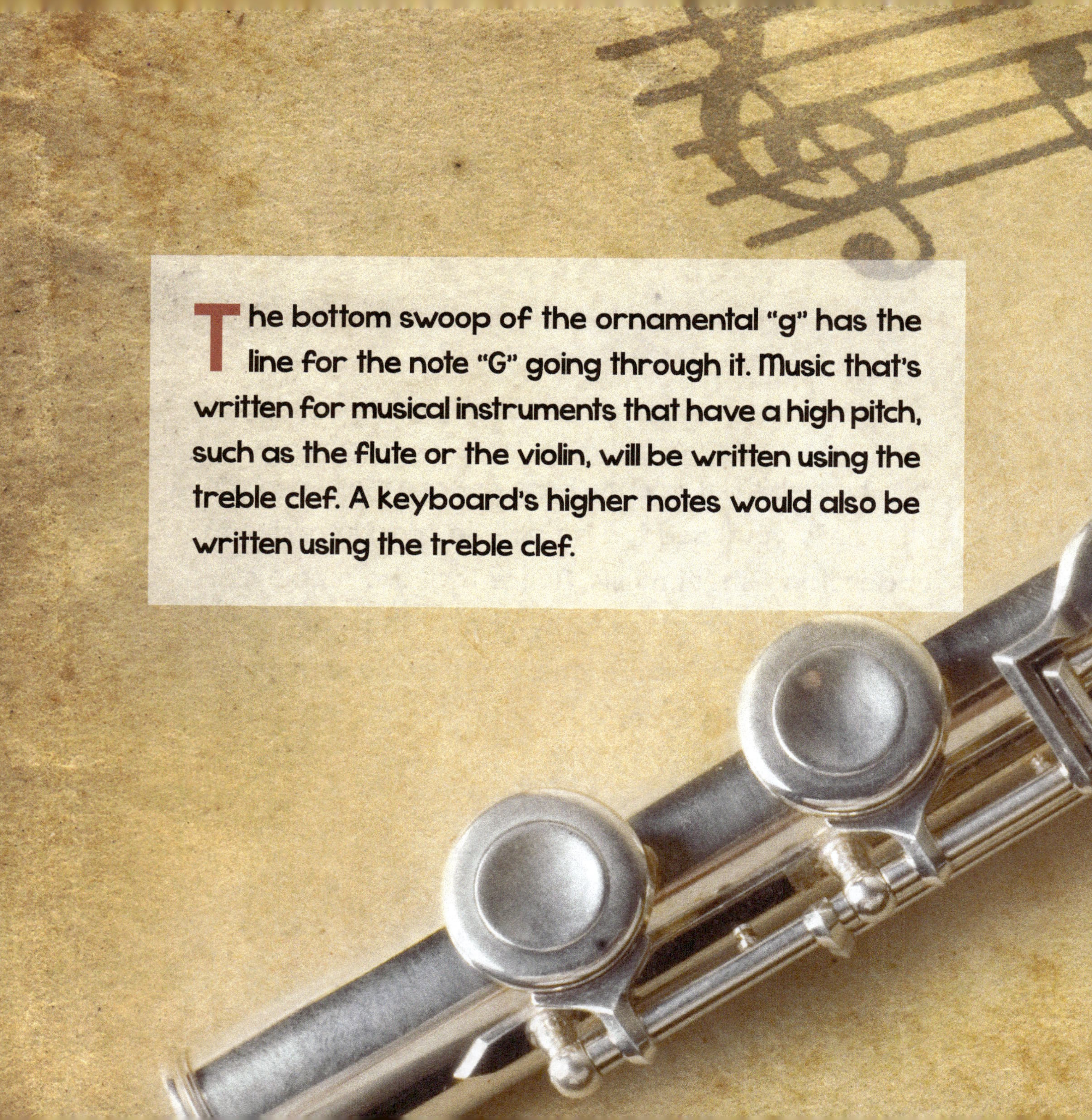

The bottom swoop of the ornamental "g" has the line for the note "G" going through it. Music that's written for musical instruments that have a high pitch, such as the flute or the violin, will be written using the treble clef. A keyboard's higher notes would also be written using the treble clef.

FLUTE

People have been using mnemonics to remember the names of the notes on the treble clef for centuries. A **mnemonic** is a phrase or sentence that helps you to remember the order of a list.

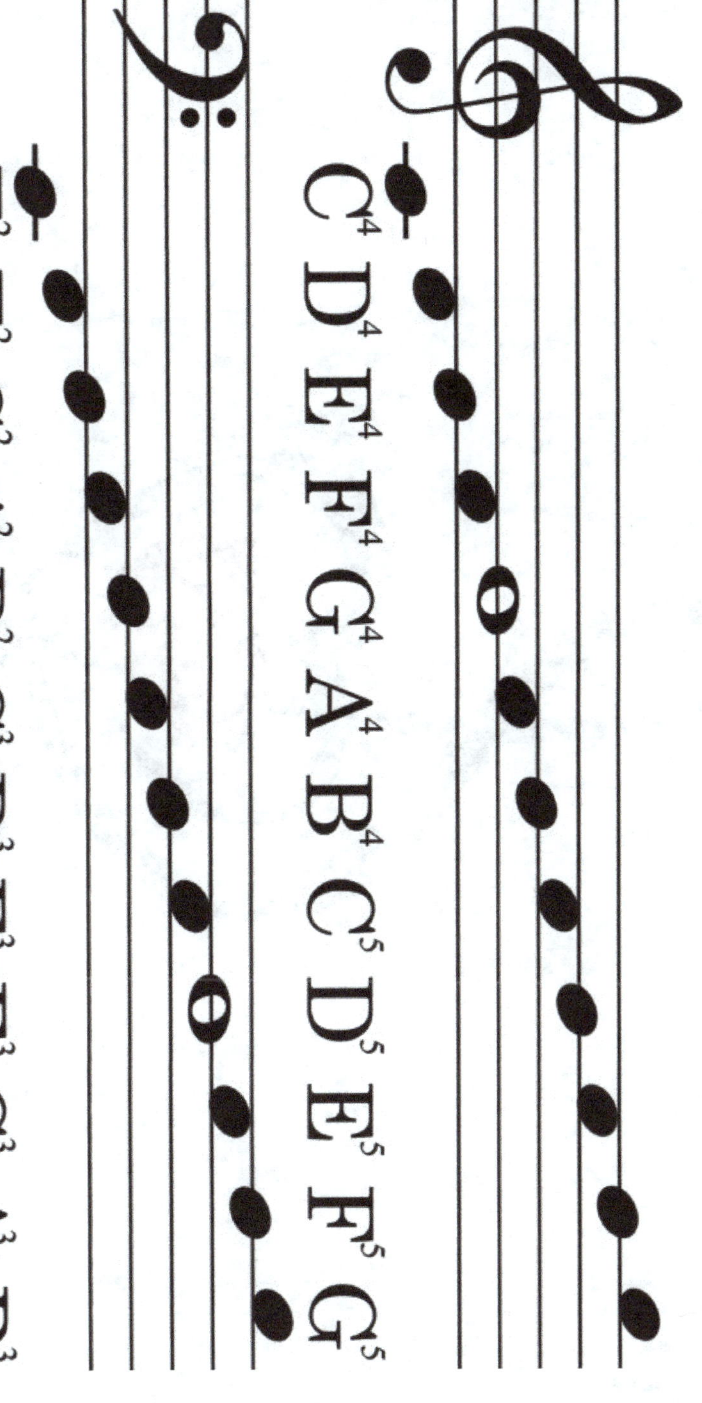

To remember the lines, which stand for the notes EGBDF, they frequently use a sentence such as "Every Good Boy Does Fine."

treble clef

The spaces stand for F-A-C-E, so those are easy to remember since they spell the word "face."

THE BASS CLEF

If you are playing a musical instrument that has a low pitch, such as a tuba or a cello, you'll be reading sheet music that's written in the bass or F clef. A keyboard's lower notes would also be written using this clef. The symbol at the left of the bass or F clef is an ornamental symbol for "f" and also the 2 dots at the right of the symbol surround the line that represents "F." The lines on the F clef stand for the letters G, B, D, F, and A.

BASS CLEFF

One common mnemonic for these letters is the sentence "Good Boys Do Fine Always." The spaces represent A, C, E, and G. Some people remember this with the mnemonic "All Cows Eat Grass."

You can always create your own mnemonic if you don't like these. Any sentence or phrase that uses the letters in order as its first letters can work.

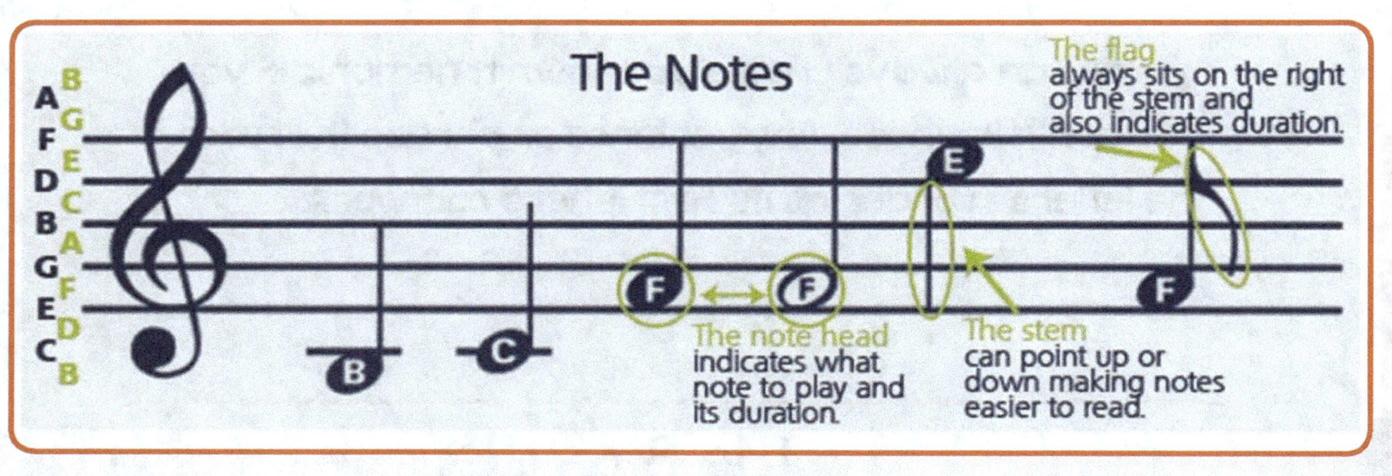

The Notes
A F D B G E C
B G E C A F D B
The flag
always sits on the right
of the stem and
also indicates duration.
The note head
indicates what
note to play and
its duration.
The stem
can point up or
down making notes
easier to read.
B
C
F
F
E
F

THE NOTES

The notes that are written on the staff tell the musician which note to play on his or her musical instrument as well as how long the sound of the note should be. To provide all this information, a note has three potential parts. It has a note head. It also has a stem and sometimes it has a flag.

THE NOTE HEAD

The head of each note will be sitting either on one of the lines or one of the spaces on the staff. At times, notes will be positioned either above or below the standard lines and spaces. When this happens, a line will be drawn either above the note or through the note so that it's clear which letter it represents.

Note head

The head of the note can be filled in black or it can be open. These represent how long the duration of the note should be.

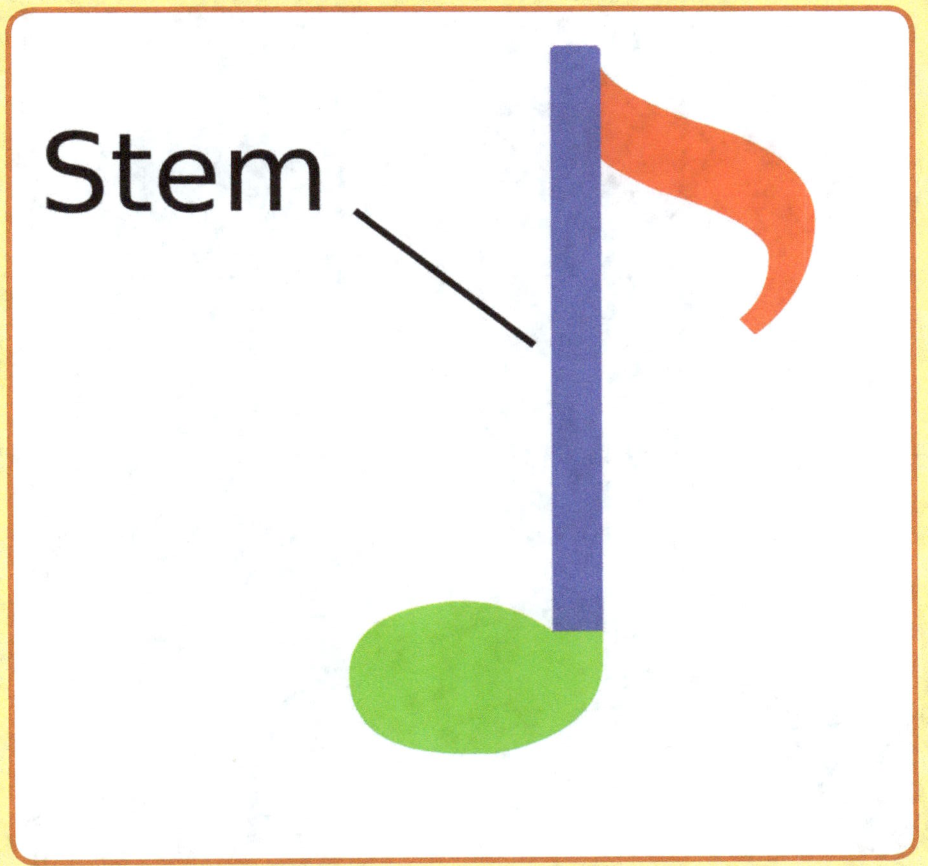

THE NOTE STEM

The thin line that is attached to the note head is called its stem. If the stem is pointing up, then it is on the right-hand side of the note.

If the stem is pointing down, then it is on the left-hand side of the note. Notice that the line for "B" is in the middle of the staff on the treble clef. In general, any notes either on or above the "B" line have stems that point down.

Those below the "B" line have stems that point up. The line's direction doesn't have anything to do with the way the note is played. Instead, it just provides a visual that helps you read the notes and keeps them neatly written on the staff.

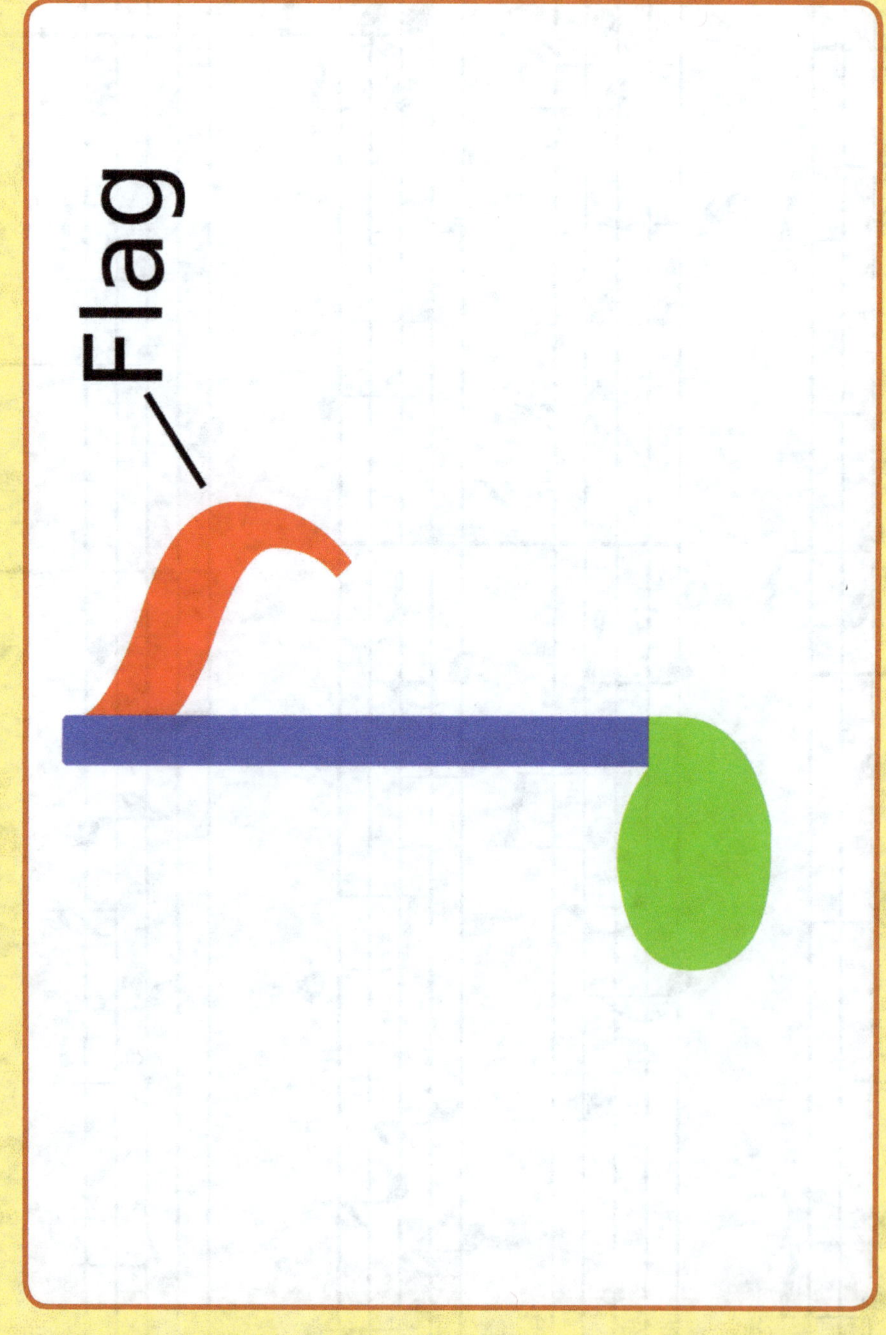

Flag

THE NOTE FLAG

The mark that is curvy and is attached on the right-hand side of a note's stem is called a "flag." The flag tells the musician how long he or she should hold a specific note. If a note has just one flag, it indicates to shorten the note. More than one flag means to make the note an even shorter duration.

FILLED AND OPEN NOTE HEADS

The head of a note tells the musician how long the note should be held. The duration is expressed in beats. For example, if the head of the note is filled in or black that means it represents just one beat. This note is called a quarter note.

If the note's head is open, it's a half note and represents two beats. If it looks like the letter "o" and doesn't have a stem it's called a whole note and gets four beats.

So, four quarter notes, two half notes, and one whole note all represent groups of notes that are played for four beats.

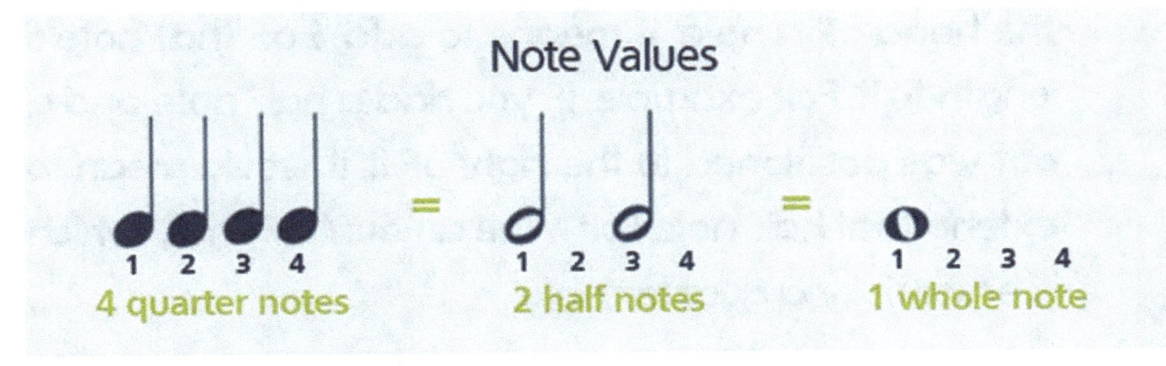

DOTS AND TIES

Filled and Open Note heads aren't the only way to show the duration of a note. If there's a dot placed after the head of a note, it means to add ½ of that note's length to it. For example, if you had a half note and a dot was positioned to the right of it, it would mean to extend that half note for ½ the amount of time, which is essentially a quarter note.

f cantabile

mein Herz?
fp

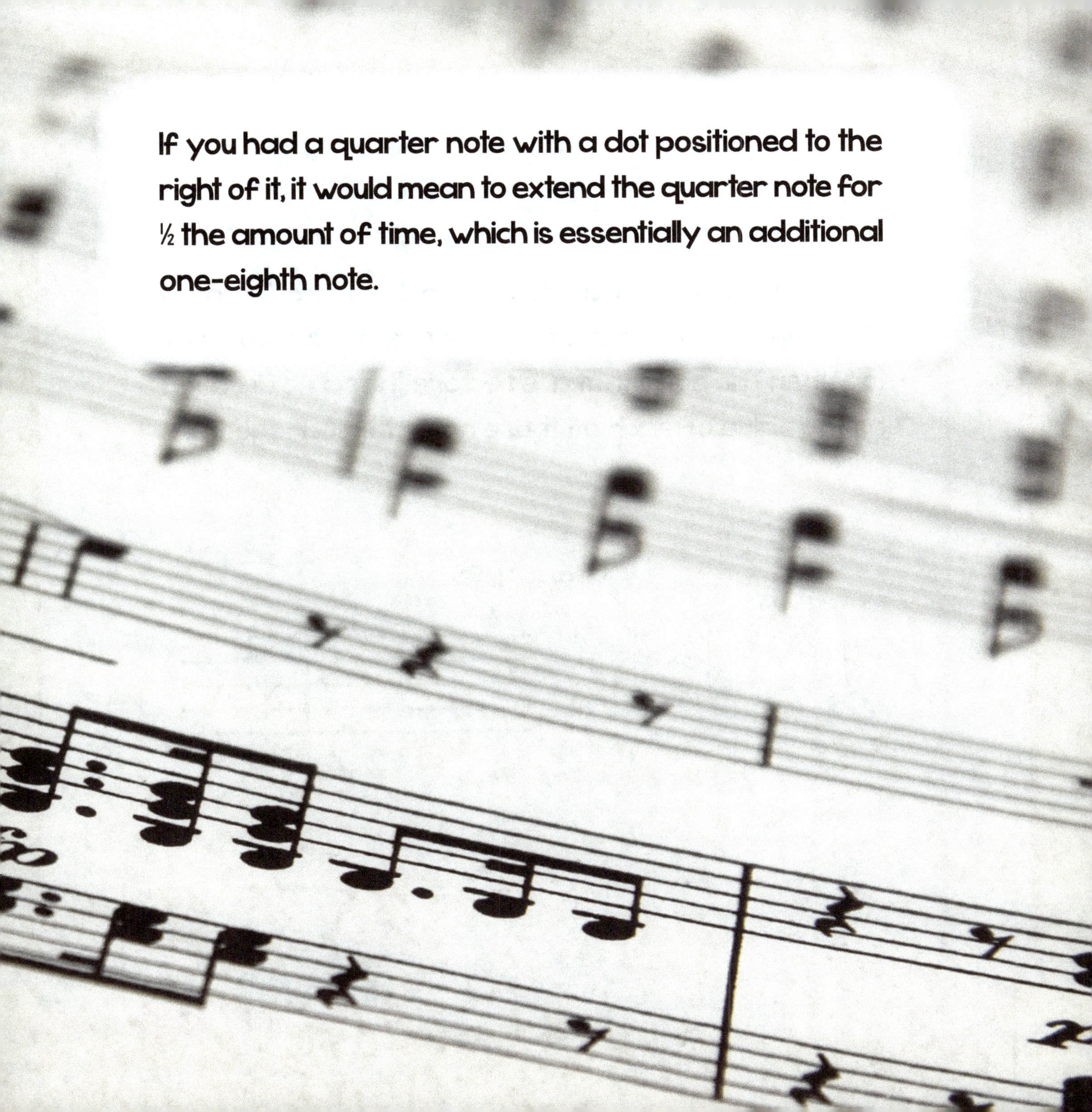

If you had a quarter note with a dot positioned to the right of it, it would mean to extend the quarter note for ½ the amount of time, which is essentially an additional one-eighth note.

A tie is another way to extend the duration of a note. A tie is a curved line that connects two notes together. The notes that are tied are the same duration as the value of each of those notes totaled together.

Dots and Ties

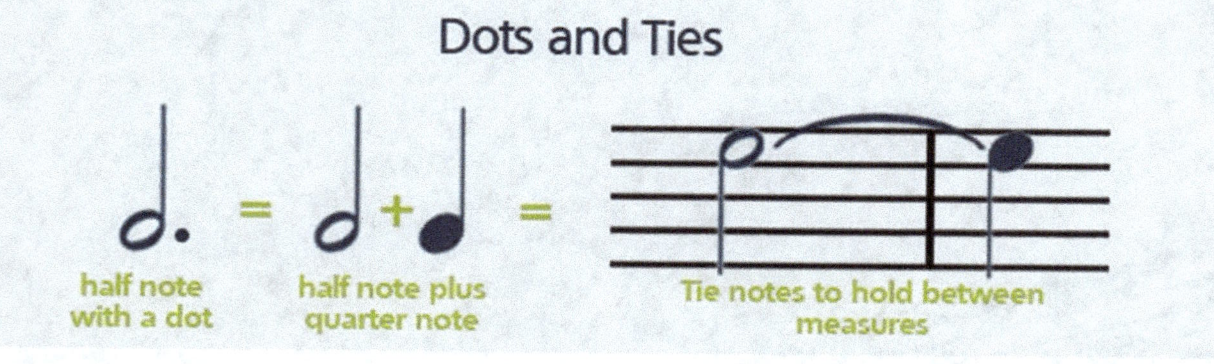

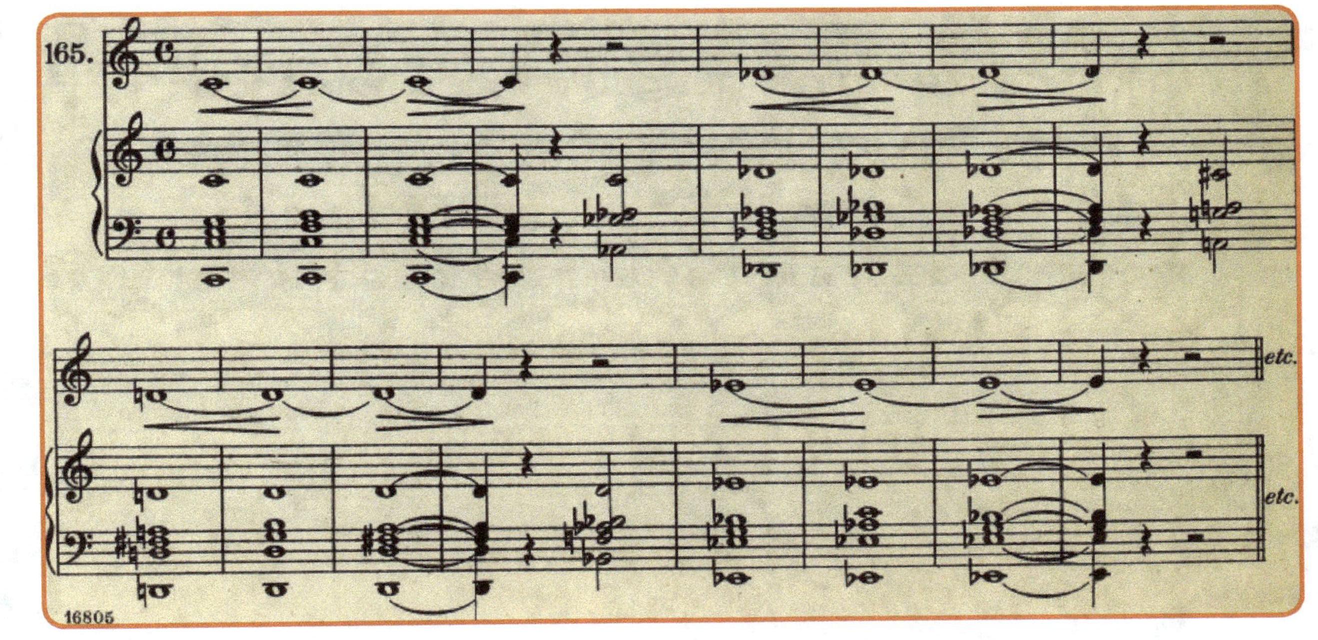

Ties are often used across bars. The bar is a vertical-line separator that helps to designate the number of beats in a particular piece of music.

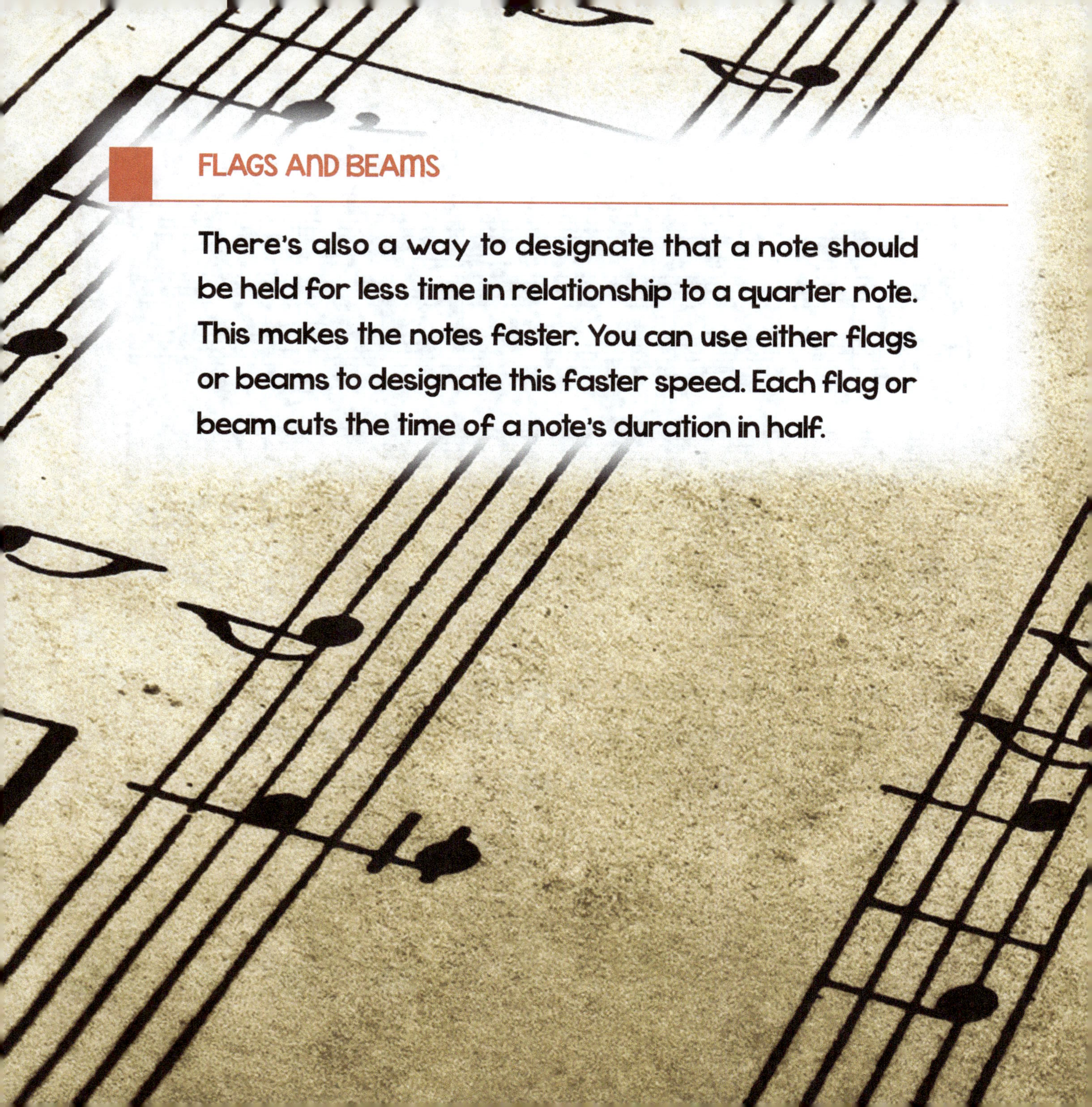

FLAGS AND BEAMS

There's also a way to designate that a note should be held for less time in relationship to a quarter note. This makes the notes faster. You can use either flags or beams to designate this faster speed. Each flag or beam cuts the time of a note's duration in half.

For example, one flag or one beam on a quarter note means ½ of that note. In other words, 4 quarter notes are equivalent to 8 eighth notes as well as 16 sixteenth notes.

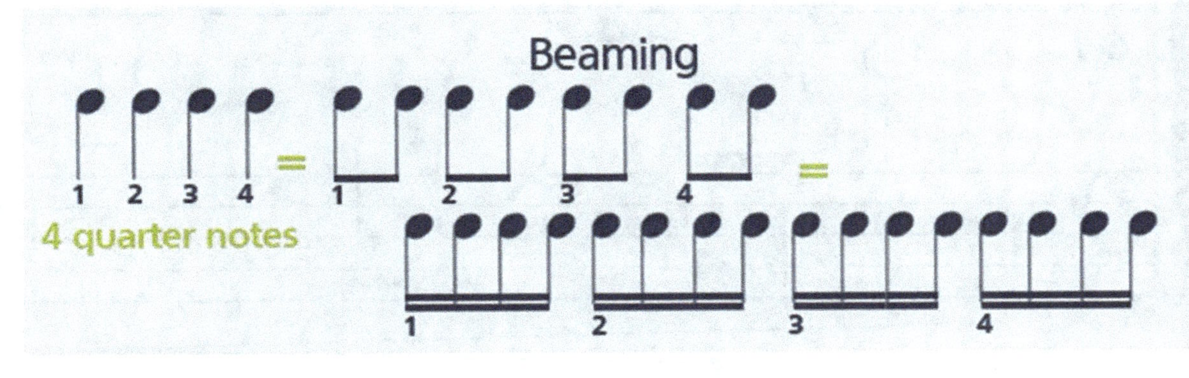

There's flexibility in how these symbols are used to make the final sheet music less filled with clutter and easier to read.

RESTS

Of course, music isn't only filled with notes. There are also pauses called rests. For example, just as a whole note represents four beats, a whole rest represents four beats where no sound is heard.

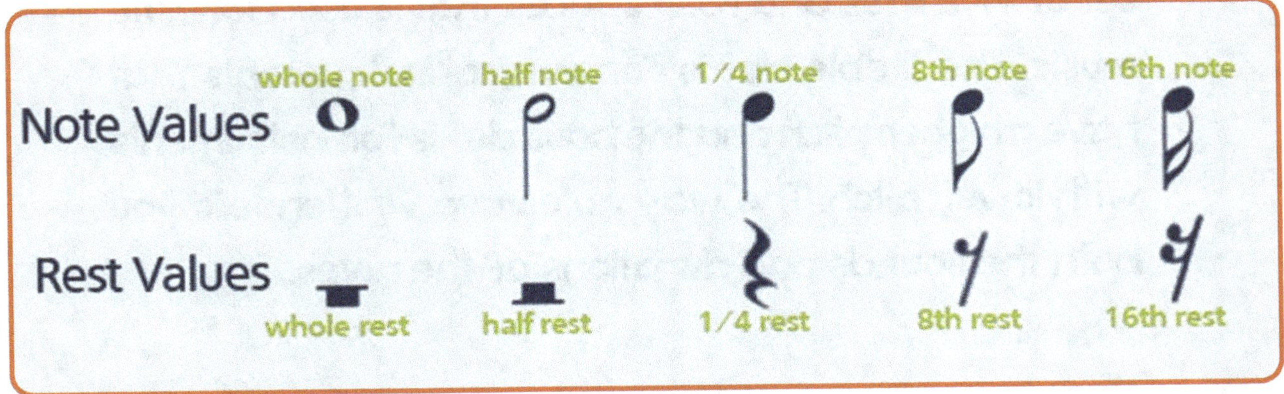

SUMMARY

There are some basic terms you need to know before you can begin to read music. The staff is a set of five lines and four spaces that is used to write music. The treble clef is for musical instruments that have a higher pitch and the bass clef is for instruments with lower pitch. The way notes are written tells you both the sounds and durations of the notes.

A MUSIC STUDENT PLAYING SAXOPHONE

Awesome! Now that you've read about the basics of how to read music, you may want to read about musical instruments in the Baby Professor book, My Mini Concierto - Musical Instruments for Kids - Music Book for Beginners - Children's Musical Instruments.

Visit
BABY PROFESSOR
EDUCATION KIDS
www.BabyProfessorBooks.com
to download Free Baby Professor eBooks
and view our catalog of new and exciting
Children's Books